IMAGES OF ENGLAND

HIGH WYCOMBE
REVISITED

IMAGES OF ENGLAND

HIGH WYCOMBE
REVISITED

COLIN J. SEABRIGHT

Frontispiece: The Little Market House, pictured around 1920, stands on the site of the ancient Hog Market, in front of the church gates.

First published in 2005 by Tempus Publishing

Reprinted in 2012 by
The History Press
The Mill, Brimscombe Port,
Stroud, Gloucestershire, GL5 2QG
www.thehistorypress.co.uk

Reprinted 2013

British Library Cataloguing in Publication Data.
A catalogue record for this book is available from the British Library.

ISBN 978 0 7524 3678 4

Typesetting and origination by
Tempus Publishing Limited.
Printed and bound in Great Britain.

Contents

	Acknowledgements	6
	Introduction	7
one	The River	9
two	Industry	15
three	Churches	27
four	Schools	37
five	Transport	51
six	Houses	61
seven	Civic Services	75
eight	Shops	85
nine	Public Houses	103
ten	Events	111
eleven	Leisure	121

The High Street seen through the arches of the Guildhall, 1928.

Acknowledgements

Nearly all the pictures reproduced here are postcards and, except where otherwise noted, most of them are over ninety years old, published in the postcard golden age between 1900, when they first came into general use, and the First World War. Many of the others were published in the thirties, when local photographers took shots of the town's suburbs spreading relentlessly over the surrounding farmland.

All are from my own collection and, I believe, now out of copyright; if not, I sincerely apologise to the copyright holders for any infringement.

I must thank the anonymous photographers and the publishers, both local and national, who produced the pictures, those who initially bought and saved them, and the postcard dealers through whom I have assembled my collection over the past thirty years.

Introduction

High Wycombe is an historic town in the steep-sided valley of the River Wye, where it cuts through the Chiltern Hills. Its official name (until 1946) was Chepping Wycombe, a name which confirms its Saxon origin, but the community existed long before that. The valley was occupied by Stone Age men and the hilltops, including Desborough Castle, were inhabited in the Bronze and Iron Ages. Later, the Romans settled beside the river and built an extensive villa with hypocaust and separate bathhouse.

It was the river that gave the start to the medieval town, providing water for all purposes, power to drive mills, and a transport route to the Thames at Bourne End. First recorded in 970 as Wicumun, High Wycombe was already a place of importance, with six mills recorded in the Domesday Book, and its church was founded soon afterwards. The town was created a borough in 1226, governed by a mayor and corporation, responsible only for the busy centre of an extensive parish.

The borough grew rich on the corn market tolls, and as the commercial centre for a large surrounding area, then later as a centre for the making of chairs, becoming in time the 'furniture capital' of the country. Its 126 acres housed a population of 5,000 in 1880, before several extensions were added, each recognising the actual area which had been or soon would be developed to meet the demands of housing and industry, and by 1935 it covered over 7,000 acres, including the surrounding hillsides, with a population of 34,000.

The cottage craft of chairmaking started in the area in the seventeenth century as a winter activity for the summer agricultural workers, using beech from the woods all around. The first small factories were set up to meet the demand for cheap chairs for the new town-dwellers after the Industrial Revolution. Initially using parts made in the woods by skilled turners known as bodgers, these factories later took on all the manufacturing processes, making a total of 4,700 chairs every day.

A guide of 1800 described Wycombe as the most handsome town in the county, while William Cobbett, who rode through it in 1822, wrote: 'Wycombe is a very fine and very clean market town, the people all looking extremely well'. Later that century, another guide remarked that:

> The place is remarkably healthy and possesses a very prepossessing appearance, the houses being generally lofty and well-built. The adjoining country is rich and fertile and agreeably diversified, the hills clad with fine hanging woods. The view of the town from the neighbouring heights is very picturesque.

In 1898, another guide noted the first expansion of the town: 'Wycombe's roofs stretch across the narrow valley of the Wye, and climb the spurs of the beech-clad hills that fence in the town to the north and south'.

In 1907, a writer reported that:

> By reason of its commercial prosperity, the beauty of its situation and the number of its inhabitants, High Wycombe is by far the most notable of all the towns in Bucks, and dwellers in the metropolis are just beginning to find out its sterling qualities as a residential centre.

These new residents brought about further expansion into the surrounding hills, but even twenty years later High Wycombe was described as 'still only a small town, and its chief industry, that of the manufacture of Windsor chairs and furniture, has not succeeded in spoiling its picturesqueness'.

In the thirties, most opinions were still complimentary about the greatly expanded town:

> The rapid growth of High Wycombe from the status of a small country town to that of an important industrial centre has been accompanied by a corresponding enlargement and improvement of local facilities for retail trade, and Wycombe is now one of the best shopping centres in the Home Counties. The town is admirably self-contained for shopping purposes, and serves as the recognised shopping centre of a large district, now linked up by its most efficient motor-bus services.

> The valley of the Wye is bordered by lofty hills up which houses are mounting, but the amount of building on the hillsides is trifling in comparison with the expanse of grasslands and woodland that delight the eye.

> England is full of villages that grew up overnight, but few can have come through the experience so painlessly and, on the whole, pleasantly, as High Wycombe.

After the Second World War, many of the smaller furniture firms faded, changed over to engineering, or were taken over by their larger rivals. This, plus mechanisation of the industry, reduced the demand for skilled woodworkers, many of whom left the area or retrained for the new factories established on the fringes of Wycombe. Much of the town centre was modernised, and opinions had changed:

> High Wycombe must have been an enchanting place, lying in its steep-sided, tree-clad valley, before modern so-called 'improvements' ruined its former beauty.

> Wycombe has suffered more than most from the destruction or mutilation of its old houses and the widening of roads; and the former dignified air of the town is now largely ruined by modern shop-fronts and tasteless conversions of old houses. The local authority, whose aim seems to be to make a second Ealing Broadway of the town, have wrought far more destruction than German bombs. St Mary Street and White Hart Street, which contained some of the oldest and most interesting properties in the town, have both been virtually destroyed.

This book makes no claim as a town history but illustrates a selection of the features which made up High Wycombe in the first half of the twentieth century, before further redevelopment, which has been described as 'the peacetime blitz that tore the heart out of the town'.

Colin J. Seabright
September 2005

one

The River

From its source in Long Meadow, West Wycombe, the River Wye fills the ornamental lakes and streams of West Wycombe Park, then enters High Wycombe between the 'pepper-boxes' in Chapel Lane, a pair of ornamental buildings at the edge of the park.

Looking back from the end of the open section, also in 1915, the terrace of small cottages opened directly on to the river bank opposite the busy road. From here the culvert passes under new buildings and much of the town centre.

Opposite below: After entering High Wycombe, the river flows mainly between factories. It was then open to public view again alongside Oxford Road, until culverted under the new dual carriageway in 1965. Looking downstream, this 1915 postcard shows the open section, with Freer's shop and post office on the corner of Brook Street.

The river appears again just before Queen Victoria Bridge, which was presented to the town in 1901 by Lord Carrington to commemorate the Queen's long reign. Below the bridge it flows between the new borough council offices and the entrance to Wendover Way and the Abbey, pictured here in 1934.

At the edge of the Rye, the river powered Pann Mill. The eighteenth-century mill buildings were bought by the corporation in 1898 and half the miller's house (behind the tree) was demolished for road widening. The mill itself and the remaining half of the house were demolished in 1971 to make way for the Abbey Way relief road.

Just below Pann Mill, in an idyllic spot on the river bank, was the official home of the borough's hayward, who was responsible for enforcing the by-laws governing the Rye. In particular he opened the gates at a set time to admit the visiting cows in the morning and to turn them out again in the early evening.

From there, the Wye flows alongside London Road, at the edge of the Rye, the town's treasured open space, pictured here in 1919, with cattle grazing in the distance.

Left: Back Stream, a tributary of the Wye, which is fed by the overflow from the Dyke, flows roughly parallel to the main river for over a mile before the two streams join together. Shortly before the confluence, Back Stream is crossed by a footbridge and ford leading to Kingsmead Road.

Below: At Wycombe Marsh, the Old King of Prussia public house stands between the main London Road (to the left of this view) and the river, with a footbridge leading to King's Mead. The pub, which advertised itself as 'The recognised halfway house between London and Oxford', was given the more patriotic name, King George V at the time of the First World War.

two

Industry

Above: Chairmaking, which started as a woodland and cottage craft, employing the plentiful local timber, grew into Wycombe's major industry. Initially, the legs and underframes were turned by bodgers, using pole lathes, in primitive shacks among the trees. Later, more solid sheds were adopted, either in the woods or in a backyard nearby, as pictured by a Wycombe photographer in the late 1890s.

Left: From the mid-nineteenth century, much of the manufacture was concentrated in small factories, where, at the industry's peak, 7,000 men produced 1½ million chairs annually in 250 workshops, of which a good example is Widgington's, which operated in St Mary Street from 1809-1919.

Above: Most of the chairs were fairly basic, mainly the Windsor type with shaped wooden seats. Others had seats of woven cane or rush matting. This was a typical rush-matting workshop; women gradually took over this part of the manufacturing process.

Right: Although most Wycombe firms made the plainer types of chair, for which there was a huge demand, towards the end of the nineteenth century some produced superior furniture for special orders, upholstered or with carved detail in classical styles. This example was made for Queen Victoria's Golden Jubilee in 1887.

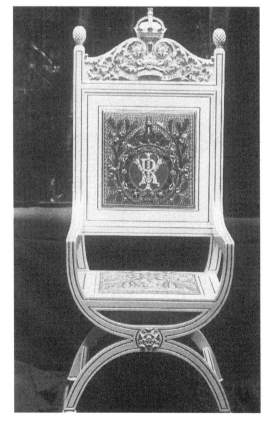

The larger factories had their own sawmills but Jonathan Plumridge's timber yard was one of several that supplied the smaller firms. His stock of tree trunks can be seen overhanging the Desborough Road pavement in 1910.

Top and above: In 1913–14 and 1919, strikes and lockouts (over rates of pay) hit the furniture industry. These two pictures, by a local photographer, show the peaceful but bored-looking pickets outside two of Wycombe's factories during the disputes.

"DOING OUR BIT"

During both world wars, most of the male workers were called up and the factories and their remaining staff were turned over to war work. Here the workers of one such factory are pictured during the First World War.

OCT. 1917.

When the industrial disputes eventually escalated into violence and vandalism, outside help was called in to assist the borough police. One of the borough policemen sent this card, noting that the Metropolitan police were the ones wearing the dark helmets, while theirs were plated.

The view from Bellfields includes much of the industrial part of the town, where the small workshops were mixed in among the terraced houses, shops and pubs. The larger firms occupied sites at the edge of the town, such as Charles Gibbons' chair factory beside the railway.

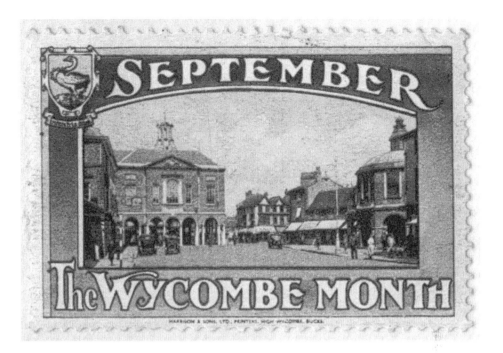

This is the stamp issued by the High Wycombe Furniture Trades Federation in 1933 to advertise Wycombe Month, a scheme to attract buyers to the town in September to place their Christmas orders. The stamps were produced in the town by Harrison's, who at that time printed all the postage stamps for Britain and most of the Empire.

A very different type of industry: agriculture in a very small way. Under an old charter, each ratepayer in the borough was entitled to graze two cows on the Rye during the day. They were led to the Rye but usually left to find their own way home when turned out by the hayward. The grazing rights were eventually withdrawn in the twenties.

Another traditional Wycombe industry was papermaking, using the waters of the Wye in the processes and for power. Here, members of the Original Society of Papermakers man a float in the town's 1911 Lifeboat Day procession. The postcard was sent by one of the men on the float, who noted that they made paper while touring the streets.

Seen here from the foot of Tom Burt's Hill in 1915, the industrial part of the town lies mainly to the left of the gasworks. Belonging to the High Wycombe Gas Light and Coke Company, the works had opened in 1848, providing gas for street lighting.

Wycombe Borough Electric Light and Power Company started supplying the town from its generating plant in Newlands in 1898 and this postcard was published for an Electrical Exhibition in 1905. By 1920, most of the factories relied on electricity to drive their machines.

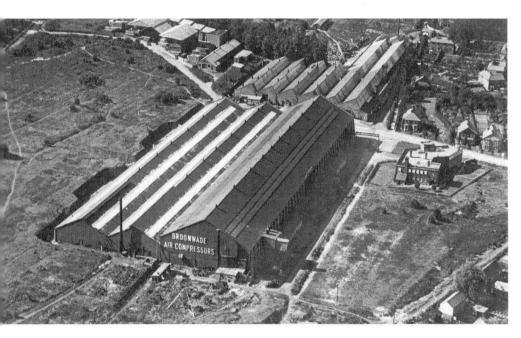

Founded by Harry S. Broom in 1898, initially in Lindsay Avenue, Broom and Wade Ltd, whose Bellfield works is pictured here in the early thirties, became one of the largest and best known manufacturers of air compressors and associated equipment.

This postcard of sewer-laying in progress in White Hart Street was sent by one of the street's shopkeepers, who wrote 'the street has been like this for three months, no traffic, no customers, no trade, thanks to our magnificently managed town'.

Stewart & Arnold Ltd's modern food-processing factory, the Newland Empire Works, was photographed in the sixties from the Octagon construction site by one of the builders there. Among other things, they developed a way of making sausage skins from seaweed, but will be best remembered locally for the delicious smell which filled the area when a gleaming tanker transferred a load of liquid chocolate.

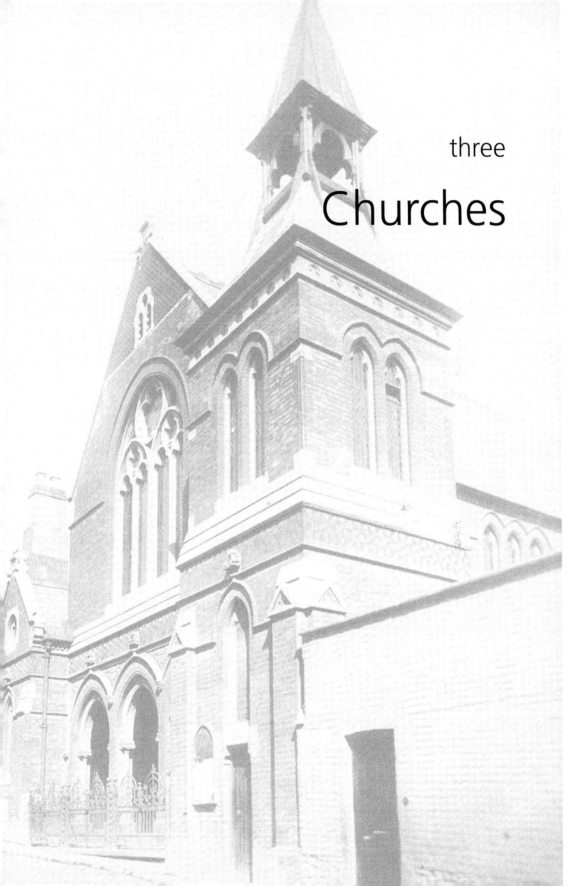

three

Churches

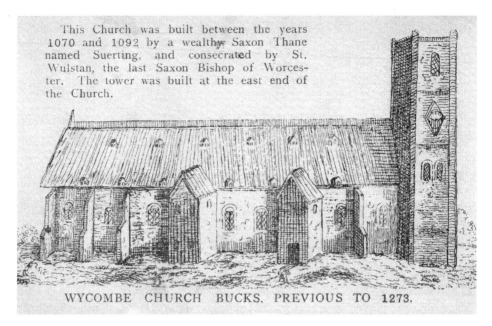

This Church was built between the years 1070 and 1092 by a wealthy Saxon Thane named Suerting, and consecrated by St. Wulstan, the last Saxon Bishop of Worcester. The tower was built at the east end of the Church.

WYCOMBE CHURCH BUCKS. PREVIOUS TO 1273.

All Saints, High Wycombe's parish church, was founded over 900 years ago and this drawing, issued as a postcard in 1930, shows how the original building is believed to have looked. Completely rebuilt in the thirteenth century with a central tower, it was altered and extended and the tower moved to its present position at the west end early in the sixteenth century, and was later subjected to Victorian restoration.

The east end of the church was photographed after a snowstorm in April 1908.

Right: The south porch of the church, seen here from under the Little Market House, was fundamentally unaltered in the restorations, and has a room over the entrance that was once reached by an internal staircase. The iron gates within the porch were originally installed at the St Mary Street entrance to Wycombe Abbey.

Below: In addition to the traditional war memorial cross on the north side of the church, another memorial to those who gave their lives in the First World War is the oak reredos behind the altar. Carved by one of the town's specialist furniture makers, it was installed in 1922.

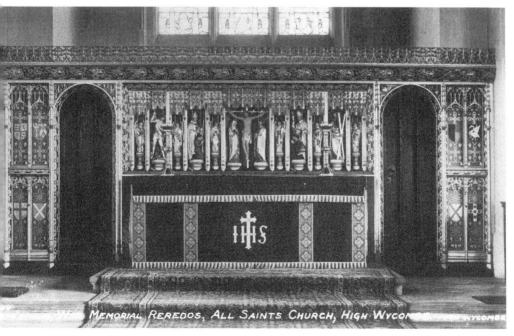

MEMORIAL REREDOS, ALL SAINTS CHURCH, HIGH WYCOMBE

The cemetery, on 4 acres of hillside overlooking the Hughenden valley, was opened in 1855, when the All Saints churchyard became full. It doubled in size by the end of the century and was further greatly extended in the twenties to meet the growing demand for space.

Established as a mission church to serve the densely populated west end of the town, the little corrugated iron chapel of St John, in Desborough Road, was erected in 1882. The larger permanent church, of red brick, was consecrated in 1903 and this postcard shows both buildings, the old church remaining in use as a parish hall.

Above and right: At the other end of the town, the then separate community of Wycombe Marsh was served by St Anne's church, built of stone and flint in early Gothic style, which stands beside London Road. The foundation stone was laid in 1858 and the finished building was consecrated three years later. The view of the exterior of the church (above) makes it appear much larger than necessary for its 100-seat interior (right).

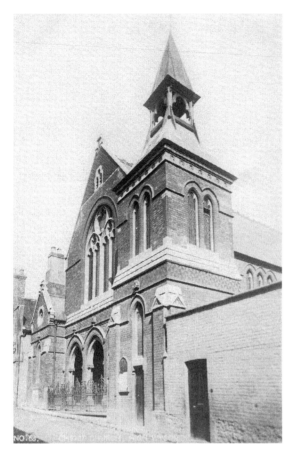

Left: Christ Church, on the east side of Crendon Street, served a separate ecclesiastical parish created in 1897. As a war memorial, a Sunday school building was erected in 1926, opposite the Town Hall in Queen Victoria Road. The church was demolished in the early sixties, long after most of its neighbours had been replaced, for further widening of the road, which had become a main entry into the town.

Below: Pictured when still fairly new, the late Victorian St Augustine's Catholic church, described as 'a handsome Gothic building', stood in Castle Street until 1957. The worshippers then moved to a new building on Amersham Hill and a block of shops was built on the Castle Street site.

Right: Hannah Ball started England's first Sunday school in High Wycombe in 1769 and inspired the local Methodists to build their first chapel in St Mary Street ten years later. They moved in 1875 to this handsome Wesleyan Chapel in Priory Road.

Below: Serving a congregation founded in 1807, Holy Trinity Chapel was built in 1851 at the far end of Easton Street, facing Pann Mill and the Rye, where its distinctive towers have remained a conspicuous landmark.

Left: The Union Baptist Chapel in Easton Street was built in 1845. This postcard view of its street frontage was printed in 1905.

Below: The interior of the chapel decorated for the harvest festival in 1907, the year before disaster befell the building.

Above: The Union Baptist Chapel
was destroyed by fire in 1908 and this
scene inside the burnt-out building is
one of several similar postcards issued
by local photographers a couple of
days after the fire.

Right: The chapel was soon rebuilt:
this postcard of the new chapel
shows posters advertising special
events there just fifteen months after
the disaster and regular services had
been restored even sooner.

GOSPEL MISSION BY MR JOSIAH NIX, MARCH 15. 1907.

In 1907, High Wycombe was included in the countrywide tour of the Gospel Mission of evangelist Josiah Nix. His mobile pulpit was parked in front of the Guildhall, on the pavement outside the Falcon inn.

In addition to services in their barracks in Frogmoor, the Salvation Army held open-air services and concerts elsewhere in the town. Here, their band – under bandmaster J. Brooker, seated behind the drums – poses outside the front door of the Town Hall in 1932.

four

Schools

High Wycombe's Royal Grammar School was established by charter from Queen Elizabeth I in 1550. Its first building in Easton Street incorporated the remains of the twelfth-century Hospital of St John the Baptist. This picture of the school building, then restored, dates from around 1875.

In 1883, new buildings were erected further back on the same site, increasing the school's capacity to 120 boys. Careful removal of the old school exposed the Norman ruins to view, and to the weather, which hastened their partial collapse. The Victorian building included a house for the headmaster, whose garden included the ruins.

A laboratory was added to the grammar school's two classrooms in the early 1900s. This photograph of a class in the laboratory, with pupil Edward Clare-Day seated in front of the new science teacher, was used as a postcard by the boy's proud parents.

In 1915, the Royal Grammar School moved from its cramped premises in Easton Street to a new site up the hill in Terriers, with adjoining playing fields and room for expansion. The whole school was involved in turning the first sods there on 6 February 1914.

The new Royal Grammar School, for 250 pupils, was formally opened on 15 July 1915, although it had already been used for a term. This postcard, published a few years later, shows the impressive neo-Georgian frontage.

Continued growth followed the increasing demand for places in the school, and the extra wings, added in the thirties, maintained the style of the first building. Later additions, however, include a large utilitarian block which hides the original building completely.

Opposite below: Funded by the proceeds of the 'beer tax', the Science and Art School was established in 1893 in Frogmoor. Later, as High Wycombe Technical Institute, it taught many of the town's furniture manufacturers and designers. In the late twenties, it moved to the Easton Street building vacated by the Royal Grammar School.

Central Schools, High Wycombe

Above: Wycombe's Central School opened in Priory Road, overlooking the heart of the town, in 1875 with one master and one mistress, each with five young assistants to teach a total of 730 pupils. By 1907, the date of this postcard, the numbers of both pupils and staff had greatly increased. The photographer attracted great interest from the boys, who had probably not seen one before.

HIGH WYCOMBE: SCIENCE & ART SCHOOLS

Wycombe Abbey was bought by the Girls' Education Company, who opened Wycombe Abbey School there in 1896, under headmistress Miss (later Dame) Frances Dove, who became the first woman to serve on High Wycombe Borough Council in 1907.

By 1907, alterations to the Abbey had provided a gymnasium, workroom, studio workshop and hall. New buildings included four boarding houses, each housing twenty-six girls, alongside Marlow Hill, seen to the left of this aerial view, which dates from the late twenties.

Above and below: The Abbey's 35 acres of grounds gave plenty of scope for outdoor recreation, including hockey and tennis, as well as boating on the lake. The girls were also encouraged to help in the grounds and had their own garden.

Above and below: Wycombe Abbey, together with adjoining Daws Hill, was requisitioned for use by the US 8th Air Force from 1942–46, and the school was temporarily disbanded. These two postcards, published by the US authorities, show the school's swimming pool, which was used by the airmen, between the Abbey and Daws Hill, and the interior of one of their 'temporary' buildings at the top of the site, which in fact remained for many years.

After the war, Wycombe Abbey School reopened but the American authorities retained Daws Hill. This view from the 1950s shows the main school building and chapel, with the modern block of Wycombe Technical College, now Buckinghamshire Chilterns University College, behind.

V. A. D. Hospital. (High School) High Wycombe.   W H A 4515.

Wycombe High School for Girls was established by the county council in 1901. Five years later it moved from temporary premises in Frogmoor to its new home in Hampden Road. This postcard was published in 1915, when their buildings had been taken over as a military hospital staffed by members of the Voluntary Aid Detachment.

Above and below: Situated high on the northern slope above the town, Godstowe School, named after the abbey which owned much of medieval Wycombe, opened early in the twentieth century. A pioneering co-educational establishment, its buildings, set in 10 acres of grounds, included the main schoolhouse (above) and three boarding houses (one of which is pictured below). Both postcards were published around 1910.

Another 1910 card illustrates the wide-ranging, still mostly rural, view from one of Godstowe's dormitory windows, with their gymnasium building on the left.

The school's spacious grounds gave ample scope for sports and games. This was the Godstowe girls' sports club in 1929.

Among the leisure facilities available to pupils of Godstowe School was horse-riding and here, in 1920, a mixed group is about to set off from outside the main school.

Shortly after the First World War, the Dames Bernardines opened St Bernard's Preparatory School alongside their convent in London Road. This postcard, one of a set of thirty published for the school in the twenties, shows the convent and, to the right, the school, on the corner of Harlow Road. They used part of the Rye, opposite the school, as their hockey field.

Opposite below: After the stone-laying, the mayor and other civic dignitaries walked in formal procession back to the Guildhall. Here they are seen passing the foot of Crendon Lane.

Above: The Borough Education Committee built an elementary school for 300 boys and 300 girls in Spring Gardens, which opened in 1909. This postcard shows the mayor laying the foundation stone of the extensive building on 9 May 1906.

London Road, Wycombe Marsh.

An infants' school was built in 1915 in Wycombe Marsh, then quite remote from the town centre. The school is on the far side of London Road, almost in the centre of this 1920s view.

Some of the school's young pupils appear in this classroom photo, taken soon after the school opened.

five

Transport

Looking up Amersham Hill, *c.* 1900. Everything stopped when the photographer set up his tripod in Crendon Street, outside the Railway Tavern. The baker's boy with his basket, the baker himself, leaning on his handcart, the man in the cart parked across the road, and all the others outside the station entrance (on the right) posed for the camera. The railway, a GWR broad-gauge branch via Bourne End from Maidenhead on the London–Bristol main line, had arrived in 1854. In the next decade it was extended to Princes Risborough, Thame and Aylesbury and in 1870 converted to standard gauge.

Opposite above: A private horse-drawn carriage conveys a small group past the Red Lion in the late 1890s. The hotel is decorated for some special occasion, possibly Queen Victoria's Diamond Jubilee celebrations, and even the lion on the portico is wearing a St George's flag.

Opposite below: Although regular coaching services through Wycombe had ceased nearly fifty years earlier, following the opening of the railway, this vehicle was brought out of retirement in 1901 for special enthusiasts' runs between Tetsworth and the Falcon inn, the original calling point for the London to Oxford coaches.

This early 1900s view of the forecourt of High Wycombe station includes several horse-drawn carriages awaiting their owners' arrival on the afternoon train from Maidenhead, where it had connected with a train from London.

Looking out from the station forecourt into Castle Street a couple of years later, a horse-bus is among the vehicles waiting outside the station gates. Opposite the station are two temperance hotels also awaiting custom from the arriving passengers, the Langham on the Crendon Street corner and Johns' at the foot of Amersham Hill.

In 1904, the 'shelf' cut into the hillside for the railway was widened to allow for the doubling of the tracks through the station for the 1906 opening of the new main line direct from London. Here, teams of navvies have begun cutting away sections of the bank prior to building the new, much higher, retaining wall behind the old one.

Even after widening, the cutting still couldn't accommodate four tracks and two platforms, so the down platform was moved 200 yards toward London, well clear of the up platform. This postcard view of the station from the Amersham Hill bridge was published around 1910.

One use of horse-drawn transport which hung on well into the twentieth century was the traditional rag and bone cart, pictured here in one of the town's new residential roads in the twenties.

THE WYCOMBE SWAN

This Motor Ambulance Boat was presented to the British Red + Society by the following places in the County of Buckingham. The Borough of Chepping, Wycombe, Hughende Bradenham, Radnage, Stokenchurch, Hazlemere, Loudwater, Flackwell Heath, Totteridg Wooburn, Bourne End, West Wycombe, Lane End, Downley, Fingest, Hedsor & Ibstone
MARCH 1916

Not a normal form of transport in the town, this boat was part of the Wycombe district's contribution to the war effort. Given a brief trial run on the Dyke, the boat's background is told on the postcard.

Members of the High Wycombe Motorcycle Club have drawn a crowd of interested spectators as they gather outside the Co-operative Society's hardware store in Paul's Row in the mid-twenties for the start of a rally. The rally marshal has momentarily stopped checking details with the owner of the first bike, in order to pose for the camera.

The Penn Bus Company ran its first buses into High Wycombe on market days in 1920. By 1928, they operated a network of routes serving the outlying parts of the town and used the one-way street on the east side of Frogmoor as a central bus station, with an office on the other side. Their fleet included a variety of makes and types of buses to suit the demand and difficulty of various routes. Some of the buses were actually made in High Wycombe, with coachwork by Wycombe Motor Bodies on chassis made by Gilford's at their Bellfield works.

Opposite below: A more conventional form of delivery was adopted by World's Stores, who had opened their High Wycombe branch in Frogmoor at the start of the twentieth century, moving to Oxford Street after the First World War. Their delivery van is pictured on a rural part of its regular round in the late twenties.

Above: In the late twenties, these two bullocks, named Dumpling and Pudding, hauled the Atora suet delivery wagon about 2,000 miles around the country as a publicity exercise. They have called in at Druce's forge in Crown Lane to be re-shod by Mr Bett, pictured between the animals.

The bus routes of the Thames Valley Traction Company reached High Wycombe later in the twenties and gradually took over the local services, in addition to operating longer-distance routes to Maidenhead, Henley, Reading and Aylesbury. Their new Wycombe Marsh garage next door to the Co-op branch in London Road is pictured around 1930.

In order to ensure that petrol was always available, the National Benzole Company operated a fleet of pump service vans, one of which was photographed around 1930 outside the petrol station on London Road, near the foot of White Hill.

six

Houses

Above: In a bid to establish himself among the English gentry, the Irish 1st Earl of Shelburne bought Loakes Manor in 1700. A later earl had the grounds landscaped, including construction of the Dyke, and in 1764 built the Rupert Gates to guard his entrance from the High Street, opposite Crendon Lane, pictured in the 1880s.

Left: A western entrance to the estate from Keep Hill was linked to the house by an avenue of lime trees. Although that entrance had long been disused, the avenue remained and is pictured on another early card.

Above and below: Lord Carrington bought the Loakes Manor estate in 1794, had the house enlarged, altered and Gothicised and renamed it, with no historic reason, Wycombe Abbey. Two early photographs from before the school was created there, issued later as postcards, show the Abbey's creeper-clad exterior and its grand entrance hall.

Also in the Wycombe Abbey estate, nearer the top of the hill, was Daws Hill farmhouse with a selection of outbuildings which were altered and extended by Lord Carrington to form Daws Hill Lodge. When he sold the Abbey to the Girls' Education Company in 1896, he and his family moved into the Lodge, seen here through its wrought-iron gates.

In 1902, a new drive was created from the house to the repositioned Rupert Gates, some way up Marlow Hill.

The Daws Hill estate included 'well-laid kitchen gardens' on the lower slopes of Tom Burt's Hill, towards the right of this 1900 bird's-eye view of the town from the hilltop. Created Marquis of Lincolnshire in 1915, Lord Carrington, who gave land there as the site for the War Memorial Hospital, sold Daws Hill in 1928 as an extension to Wycombe Abbey School.

The Priory, a large sixteenth-century house in the centre of High Wycombe, facing the church, had been refaced with brick 300 years later. The creeper-covered building is pictured in its last years as a private house, for in the early thirties it was converted into a block of shops, including Halfords, who are still there today.

Above: Many of the High Street houses were rebuilt for the town's wealthier citizens in the eighteenth century, a peak period in the town's prosperity, and a century later the street was still mainly residential. Even in 1905 the south side was outwardly unaltered, except for the Cheap Stores, but most of the houses then held the offices of solicitors, accountants or architects.

A healthier working-class district was created in the 1850s at Saffron Platt, then outside the borough boundary, between the new railway line and London Road. Around fifty years later, Saffron Road is seen with Housden's corner shop at the top and the side of Holy Trinity church at the bottom of the hill.

Opposite below: To the west of the town centre, Newland, the artisans' area, became an unhealthy slum due to the primitive sanitary facilities and marshy subsoil. Clearance was proposed in 1920 but Albert Lambourne, who took this photo, still lived there in 1924. Ten years later, a slum clearance order moved the occupiers to a new estate established by the council at Castlefield.

One side of London Road was built up after the road was included in the borough's extended boundary of 1880. In the 1890s many business owners moved out of the town centre into these large villas facing the Rye.

Although mostly outside the borough until 1901, Amersham Hill became a popular address for the wealthiest businessmen and professionals, who built large, individually designed mansions in the fresher air of the open countryside looking down on the town. Bearing a 1905 postmark, the view on this card includes probably the most opulent of these houses.

These houses in the upper part of Priory Road were only five years old when this postcard was sent in 1907.

In the 1880s Wycombe expanded westward through the suburb of Desborough, with terraces of working-class houses interspersed with corner shops, chair workshops and the inevitable public houses. This 1912 view of Green Street also includes, under the third shop-blind, the local post office.

Development spread rapidly along the valley and reached Desborough Park Road in Victoria's reign. This view of the road, which was published before the First World War, looks down the hill across the dip of the Wye valley and beyond it to West Wycombe Road and the open slopes below Downley.

Although the town's growth had reached Desborough Avenue by 1900, development was then confined to the valley and only later spread up the hill. This view of the upper part of the road in the thirties includes the new pub on the corner of Deeds Grove and, in the distance, the allotments and smallholdings created on the Downley hillside.

Beyond the well–developed area of Desborough, Wycombe Council started a new estate to house those evicted from the town's clearance areas in 1934. Building started around Spearing Road, backing onto Castlefield Wood near the ancient earthwork of Desborough Castle, alternatively known as the Roundabout.

By 1935, development had spread into the valley of the old Booker Lane below Desborough Castle. From this hillside viewpoint, one can see over the new houses and Desborough to Bellfield (top right) and beyond, into the Hughenden valley.

Oakleigh, a house in Totteridge Avenue, in the late twenties. Building started in Totteridge Avenue around 1900, when it was little more than an unfenced track from the Gordon Road railway bridge up the hillside to Wheeler's Field, where the brewers had grown their hops.

Above and below: Development of Micklefield began in 1930 with these houses along the old track to Micklefield Farm. Opposite the houses was a rifle range alongside the new road, which gave the name to the nearby Rifle Butts pub in London Road. Both sides of the road were fully built up a couple of years later and by 1934 development extended beyond the old farm and reached the top of the valley, where Herbert Road was under construction below Gomms Wood, some 200ft higher than the entrance to the estate from the main road.

Construction of the Bowerdean Farm Estate started in the mid-twenties on the farm's lower fields. By 1933, Bowerdean Road extended up the valley at the bottom of this view for half a mile towards Terriers. Totteridge Road climbs the hill on the far side of the valley towards Totteridge.

A couple of years later and onward extension of Bowerdean Road had come to a halt, but Underwood Road had been built parallel to it on the valley's western slope, under Lucas Wood. It was another twenty years before the roads reached the hilltop near Terriers church, visible in the top left corner of the photograph.

seven

Civic Services

Closing the view at the end of the High Street is the 1757 Guildhall, containing the Council Chamber, raised on slender stone pillars above the open area where the town's prosperous weekly corn market was once held. This photograph dates from the thirties, when the market area was in use for more modern retail purposes.

Wycombe's cottage hospital, formally called the High Wycombe and Earl of Beaconsfield Memorial Cottage Hospital, opened in 1875 at the top of Priory Road, off Amersham Hill. Initially, it had two wings and a veranda giving views over the town. A third wing was added in 1891 and at the end of the nineteenth century, when this picture was taken, it offered twelve beds and two cots.

The cottage hospital was replaced in 1927 by the High Wycombe and District War Memorial Hospital. It was built, on land given by the Marquis of Lincolnshire, in memory of the 500 local men who died in the First World War. Seen here from the Barracks Road entrance, it opened with facilities for thirty-five patients.

Already recognised as a training school for nurses, in conjunction with the Royal Bucks Hospital in Aylesbury, the hospital was extended to meet the demands of the rapidly growing town. This view, from the lower slopes of Tom Burt's Hill, was published in the mid-thirties, when the hospital's capacity was fifty-five patients.

The fire brigade is seen here attending a shop fire in Crendon Street in May 1906. Postcards like this, which went on sale very soon after the event, formed a sort of pictorial supplement to the local paper.

Above and below: Founded in 1868, the Borough Volunteer Fire Brigade here proudly displays the new manually pumped, horse-drawn engine in 1888 in Spring Meadow, near the little fire station at Temple End, originally built to house the previous engine which had initially been kept in the church porch. At the end of the century they moved, with a steam-powered pump, to a new fire station in Priory Road, where their first fully mechanical engine was based from 1920. Early in the Second World War, the local brigade was absorbed into the National Fire Service, when part of the team posed with a powerful modern trailer pump outside the fire station (below).

Above: Queen Victoria Road, which followed the line of the old carriage drive to the Abbey, was given to the town by Lord Carrington in honour of Queen Victoria's Diamond Jubilee, to house the civic buildings. The first to be built was the Town Hall, opened on 12 October 1904; this postcard view of the frontage was posted the following week.

The next civic building constructed in Queen Victoria Road was the borough's Municipal Offices, including a new Council Chamber, erected in 1932 facing the Town Hall and extending almost to the river, just below Queen Victoria Bridge. Mature trees on the river bank were retained and the ground there attractively landscaped.

The town's public library, which replaced a privately financed free library established in 1875 in Oxford Street and later in Church Street, was built next door to the Town Hall in 1933. The building also incorporated an art gallery and a museum devoted mainly to the chair industry.

Opposite below: A wintry view of Queen Victoria Road from the High Street, captured by a local photographer in April 1908, when the Town Hall was still the only building in the road. Part of Wycombe Abbey is just visible at the far end of the road, between the trees.

The main post office moved around 1900 from the High Street to the ornate building to the right of this view of Easton Street. At that date, they offered an excellent service, opening from 7.00 a.m. until 9.30 p.m. on weekdays and from 8.00 a.m. to 10.00 a.m. on Sunday mornings, with seven sub-post offices around the town offering slightly shorter hours.

In 1934, the post office moved into new premises in Queen Victoria Road, joining the other civic buildings. Pictured a couple of years later across the attractive library garden, the Christ Church Sunday school then stood between the new post office and the Municipal Offices at the far end of the road.

The County Police built this police station in Hughenden Road in 1870. When this photograph was taken in 1915, the force, under Superintendent Charles Summers, consisted of an inspector, five sergeants and twenty-six constables. The smaller, but staunchly independent, Borough Police, founded in 1839, with its old station in Newlands, was then under Head Constable Oscar Sparling, who doubled as the borough's Weights and Measures Inspector. Obstinately maintaining its status, the Borough Police remained separate from the County Police until 1947, though at times of stress, such as the violence during the chairmakers' lockout, they were forced to call on outside assistance.

Left: The old watch house in Noyce Lane was the base for the nightwatchmen of the Borough Police. It was built in the sixteenth century at the end of a short row of cottages backing onto the churchyard, where the jettied upper floors almost met those opposite. The whole block, the other end of which was the Black Boy pub, was demolished for the widening of Church Street in the thirties.

Below: In 1935, the local County Police moved to a new headquarters just beyond the Town Hall, completing the line-up of civic buildings in Queen Victoria Road. The new police station included offices, cells and accommodation for unmarried officers.

eight

Shops

Above and below: Wycombe's general retail market assembled under and around the Little Market House. Pictured in 1905, some traders have set up their stalls in the High Street, a practice which soon spread further along the road. By 1934, the weekly market reached well past the Red Lion to the corner of Corporation Street, but still only on the north side of the road.

THE MARKET, HIGH WYCOMBE, 2.

In 1930, the High Street was still fairly quiet except on market days and the road was wide enough for a line of parked vehicles and all the through traffic, including an open-staired Thames Valley double-decker bus. The sunny side of the street held mostly small shops either side of the Red Lion.

Corporation Street was cut through into the High Street in 1901; it was intended to house essential public buildings, starting with the post office, but they refused to move from Easton Street. The two impressive new corner buildings housed Capital & Counties Bank Ltd (left) and Davenport Vernon & Co. Ltd (right), who were ironmongers and household appliance merchants.

Towards the far end of Easton Street, these three businesses were among a small group of shops serving East Town. William Tracy's grocery store, on the right, had a separate fruit and vegetable department in the adjacent garden and offered a delivery service by a young boy with a handcart. At the other end of the small block of shops, the window of Ada Petty's toy shop has proved a great attraction for a passing schoolboy.

In 1907, W.H. Smith's on the Crendon Street corner of the High Street offered a large selection of postcards, then at their peak of popularity, displayed on a rack in the doorway.

All of the left side of Crendon Street, up the hill to the station, including the Friends Meeting House, was demolished in 1930 for road widening. A unified block of shops, in neoclassical style, replaced the assortment of old buildings in Crendon Street and by 1933 most of them were occupied by a wide variety of retail businesses, with offices on the upper floors.

Established in 1897, the High Wycombe Co-operative Society's main store in Paul's Row, behind the Guildhall, is seen here a few years later. The shop assistants and juniors are standing on the pavement with the fruit and vegetable display, under the hanging poultry and sides of meat. Even their delivery horse is included in the photo, posing in the archway leading from the stables behind the store.

113. White Hart St. High Wycombe.

Above: This 1931 view of White Hart Street, looking towards Newlands, includes the shops on the south side, mostly in converted houses at least 300 years old. All, including the White Hart pub, were replaced in 1970 by the Octagon shopping centre. In the distance, Aldridge's building carried the permanent fittings for their famous Christmas displays.

Right: This advertising card issued by Aldridge's shows their traditional, if unhygienic, display of Christmas poultry and game covering the building in 1930. James Aldridge had started the business in White Hart Street around 1890, initially as a greengrocery.

Telegraphic Address: " Rabbits, High Wycombe."   Telephone No. 150.

FROM

J. ALDRIDGE,

Wholesale Fruiterer, Commission Agent, &c.

WHITE HART STREET,
HIGH WYCOMBE.

Awarded the Cup presented by Farmers for Best Show in High Wycombe, Christmas, 1937.
Photo : Goodearl.

Wycombe's Own Store

Meet your friends at MURRAYS the Popular Store, among people who recognise Good Value.

Easy Selection Shopping in all Departments.

Use the Newlands Car Park next to the Store

Above: Prestwood cattle–dealer Cornelius Stevens opened his first butcher's shop there around 1890, with a High Wycombe branch in White Hart Street shortly afterwards. This postcard shows the indoor Christmas display which won them the cup for best show in High Wycombe in 1937.

Left: Murray's, established in 1921, expanded their Walk Round Store in White Hart Street into the site of the Primitive Methodist Chapel in 1952. The store is shown here in a Murray's advertisement four years later. Known as Wycombe's Own Store, it became the largest department store in Buckinghamshire after further expansion into the new Octagon shopping centre in 1971.

The International Tea Company opened their High Wycombe store in White Hart Street in the 1890s. In the twenties, they moved along the road to a larger shop, pictured in 1928 with the smartly dressed assistants and cashier in front of the windows.

A busy day in White Hart Street in 1911 is viewed from outside the White Hart pub, looking towards the Guildhall and the High Street. This short street could provide all the family's regular shopping requirements, with three grocers, three butchers, two greengrocers, two chemists, two drapers and four public houses.

Opposite above: The sixteenth-century former Chequers public house building on the corner of White Hart Street and Church Street was occupied for over eighty years, from 1870, by Dring's outfitters and linen drapery. The historic building was allowed to decay in the sixties, and was later demolished and replaced by a modern replica.

Opposite below: Around the corner in Church Street, in 1935 Woolworths had recently opened their new store just along from their other bazaar in Queens Square. Facing Woolworths, Joe Lyons' new café was built on the site of the fourteenth-century Old Guildhall which had been superseded by the first Guildhall in the High Street.

NO. 54. — WHITE HART ST., HIGH WYCOMBE.

JOHN R. DRING.

BUTCHERS Sands

E Sweetland High Wycombe

Church St

Pictured in the early 1900s, Henry Cox had opened his hairdressing salon in Church Street ten years earlier, advertising 'Haircutting, singeing, shampooing, etc.; hot and cold baths always ready; only first-class artistes engaged; the finest hairdressing saloon in the county'.

Above: Posted in 1915, this postcard shows Queens Square, looking towards Church Street. The view includes two of the five boot and shoe shops then in the square. Busby's (under the blind) faces Hilton's, next to which is Thomas Clarke's toyshop (behind the lamp-post). Lansdale's Cash Chemists, to the right, also included a veterinary department.

Right: The Fifty Shilling Tailors, established soon after the First World War to provide affordable suits for returning servicemen, didn't open their High Wycombe branch in Queens Square until the thirties. The shop is seen here in 1939, with Woolworths next door. The premises were previously owned by tailor James Peace and the gables still carry the legend 'Hen and Chickens', the sign of the tailor.

Left: Mrs Bateman, wife of a chair manufacturer, opened her millinery shop at No. 18 Queens Square around 1880. This photograph was taken thirty years later; the premises became an optician's of the same name after the First World War.

Below: Looking through Queens Square into Frogmoor in 1925, Boots, who had opened their first shop in the town around 1910, display the familiar logo on the shop's sunblinds and carry a sign announcing National Insurance Dispensing. The tall chimney behind the shops of Frogmoor belongs to one of the chair factories.

8 ... Queens Square and Frogmore, High Wycombe

On the east side of Frogmoor, the trees had been recently pollarded in 1905. At the edge of the view, Prosser's Bristol House drapery is next to the Hare and Hounds, followed by the Frogmoor Coffee Tavern and Popp's newsagents. The pub closed around 1920 and all the pictured buildings, except Popp's, were rebuilt by 1960, and then again for the Chilterns shopping centre.

Jacob Popp, seen in the doorway of his Frogmoor newsagent's and tobacconist's shop, was persecuted by the local authority for daring to open on Sundays. From 1901 to 1908, he appeared in court every Monday, where he was fined a nominal sum for the offence.

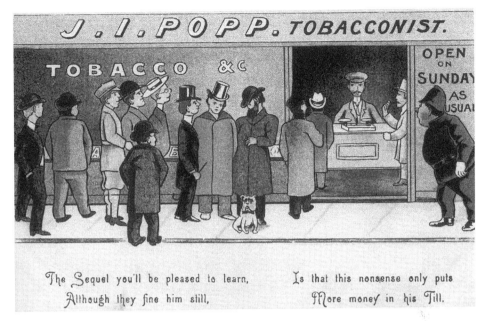

J.J. POPP. TOBACCONIST.

TOBACCO &c

OPEN ON SUNDAY AS USUAL

The Sequel you'll be pleased to learn,   Is that this nonsense only puts
Although they fine him still,   More money in his Till.

Popp cashed in on the publicity and issued a set of six humorous cards with cartoons and verses telling his story; this is the last card in the set.

Still flourishing today after over 110 years, Isaac Lord's ironmongery business was established in 1892 at No. 178 Desborough Road, supplying tools and fitments to most of the chairmakers. In 1901, they moved along the road to premises at No. 202, on the right of this photograph, and in the thirties modernised and expanded into the shop next door. Finally, in the seventies, they moved into new buildings across the road and their old shop was demolished.

Thomas Reed sent this postcard of his shop at No. 196 Desborough Road in 1916. Without refrigeration, his stock of fish and meat was kept fresh and cool by natural ventilation, with the front and side of the shop open to the elements.

William Morton's Desborough Road shop window is crammed full of boots and shoes in the mid-twenties, with many more hanging in the doorway, at prices from 1s 11d to 5s 11d per pair.

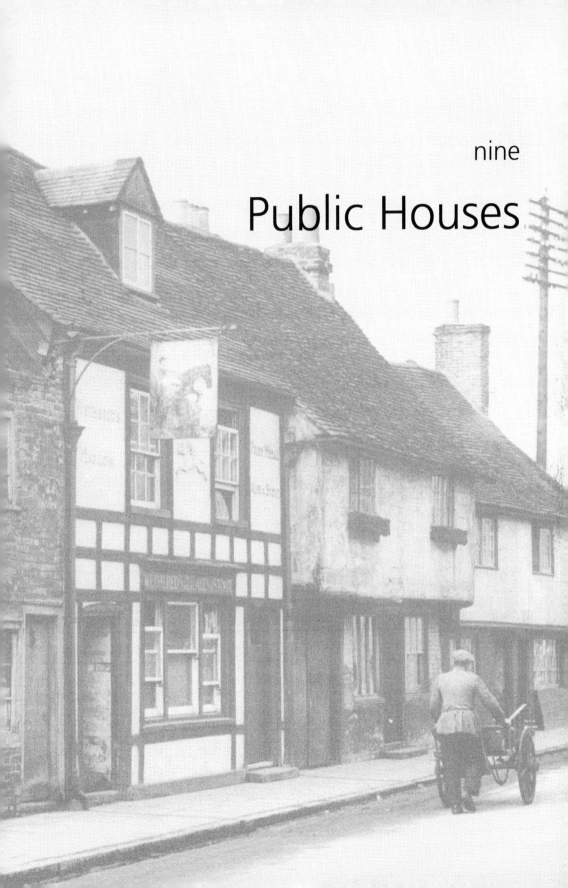

nine

Public Houses

This view of the High Street, a 1772 engraving which was issued as a postcard in 1910, includes signs for inns which no longer exist. Most importantly, on the right, the Antelope, which a few years later became the base for the Royal Military College, under Lieutenant General Le Marchant, until it moved to Sandhurst in 1812.

Starting from Frogmoor, the first part of Hughenden Road was developed in the early years of Victoria's reign. This card of the Beaconsfield Arms, at the foot of Hamilton Road, was posted in 1905 by the occupants of the house on the far left.

Above left: Pictured in 1902, the Wheatsheaf inn, almost next door to the Little Market House, is an ancient timber-framed building, partly restored but with its original oversailing top storey. Damaged by fire the following year, it was then converted into a shop.

Above right: The frontage of the Falcon, next to the Guildhall, is a familiar feature of the High Street but this postcard shows the creeper-covered courtyard at the older rear of the inn.

Right: The most noted feature of the grand Red Lion Hotel was the painted wooden lion on its portico, carved locally in 1820. Pictured in the late thirties, the hotel advertises the Winter Garden, which was added, together with a Georgian Banqueting Room, in 1934.

The Black Swan, in a back street in the densely populated area of Newlands, was destroyed by fire in 1905. A policeman is holding back onlookers shortly after the blaze.

A mother and her young son and daughter lost their lives in the disaster. Part of their funeral procession, with an escort of brass-helmeted firemen, is pictured making its way through the crowds thronging Oxford Street. The victims were buried at St Margaret's church, Tylers Green.

Pictured in 1927, with a solitary policeman on point duty at the High Street corner, the Black Boy inn projected into Church Street. Only a few years later, the pressure of traffic here prompted its demolition, together with the adjoining ancient cottages beside the churchyard.

Above: A traffic jam outside the Ship in the narrow part of Oxford Road, beside the river, isn't helped by a flock of sheep being driven into the town.

Left: The Carrington Arms, further along Oxford Road, dates from the mid-Victorian growth of the town towards West Wycombe. This postcard was written by landlord Robert Green around 1930.

A few years earlier, the regulars of the Carrington Arms had assembled outside for an outing; some of them are already seated on a furniture cart parked in the road. The photograph was taken from the other side of the Wye. The passage between the buildings served Carrington Cottages, which were behind the pub.

The Horse and Jockey, together with its neighbours in St Mary Street, was threatened under a slum clearance order in 1935. After a long battle between the council's Sanitary Inspector, who described the pub as 'putrid', and other witnesses, who called it 'one of the best beer-shops in the district' and said that 'demolition would be a public scandal', it was reprieved until the construction of the inner relief road thirty years later.

ten

Events

Above and below: In 1906, a large number of soldiers descended on High Wycombe for training exercises at the barracks at the foot of Tom Burt's Hill. This view from the hillside shows the marquees and hundreds of conical tents erected to accommodate them on land belonging to the Daws Hill estate. While in the town, the troops had time to spare and in the photograph below, many of them are simply standing about or relaxing in the High Street.

Above left: The result of the 1906 election, in which Thomas Herbert was returned as the Liberal MP for the Wycombe constituency, was announced from the portico of the Red Lion to the crowds below.

Above right and right: An annual event in Wycombe's social calendar was Lifeboat Day, with a carnival procession through the town to the Rye, where, in some years, a borrowed lifeboat was launched on the Dyke. These pictures, from the 1907 event, show Britannia's carnival float and a character from one of the tableaux.

Sunday schools reached their peak of popularity in the 1900s, with over 500 members at the Primitive Methodist Chapel in White Hart Street alone. Their annual Whitsun procession around the town, led by a brass band, was photographed in Queen Victoria Road from the window of Edward Sweetland's White House Studio in the High Street.

High Wycombe's celebrations of King George V's Coronation in 1911 included mass singing by children from all of the town's schools. The groups, with their individual banners and placards, gather in the High Street, seen from the Guildhall.

Opposite below: The official proclamation of the accession of King George V was made from the Guildhall by the mayor, Walter Birch, on 9 May 1910, before a guard of honour including members of the High Wycombe Volunteer Fire Brigade.

The singing was led from the Red Lion portico and many of the children have assembled where they can see the conductor, who is standing beside the lion.

The Marquis of Lincolnshire's heir, Viscount Wendover, an officer in the Royal Horse Guards, was killed in battle in France in May 1915. A military funeral was held in High Wycombe the following month; the hearse is seen here in Easton Street, near the foot of Crendon Street.

During the First World War, High Wycombe's population doubled with soldiers billeted in the town, where they were drilled in the recreation grounds, the artillery exercised in Daws Hill Park and the engineers trained in bridge-building across the Dyke. In July 1918, military sports competitions were held in front of large crowds on the Rye.

Wycombe traditionally weighs the incoming and outgoing mayors to check whether they have 'grown fat at the ratepayer's expense' during their year of office. The weighing, like this one in the twenties, is performed publicly under the Guildhall, using scales hired from a fairground guess-your-weight stall, and the gathered townsfolk jeer any who have put on weight.

McIlroy's store in Church Street and its neighbour, corn merchant G.E. Stevens, display loyal decorations to celebrate George V's Silver Jubilee in 1935. McIlroy's, a branch of a Reading firm and one of the first department stores, was established here in 1899. After its closure in 1953, Marks & Spencer took over the site.

Frogmoor was lit up in celebration of the 1937 Coronation of George VI. The scene was photographed by Henry Blackwell, proprietor of the chemist's shop there. The panels of light surround the office windows of the Wycombe Borough Electric Light and Power Company.

Troops were again billeted in High Wycombe during the Second World War. No. 232 Battery of the 67th Medium Regiment of the Royal Artillery is pictured in June 1941, prior to embarkation for the North Africa campaign.

eleven

Leisure

One of High Wycombe's Scout groups preparing to set off for their Easter Camp in 1911. Their smart new trek cart does not yet appear to be loaded but in other respects they are fully prepared – with a large first-aid box.

The Grand Cinema in Desborough Road was opened in 1913 and this postcard view was posted soon afterwards.

Tom Burt's Hill, named after the labourer who dug up a hoard of money there in 1729, was bought by Wycombe Council in 1937 to preserve it as an open space for the benefit of the town. Mostly open grassland, commanding views across the town centre, a narrow belt of woodland above the meadow offers secluded paths with glimpses of the town between the trees.

Frogmoor, once a private garden, was laid out and presented to the town in 1877. Its most noted feature was the ornamental fountain, and a popular leisure activity was just sitting around the stone base of the fountain, watching the world go by.

Left: In Oxford Street, facing
Frogmoor, the Electroscope
Cinema Theatre opened in 1912.
Its ornately decorated frontage
is pictured in the late twenties,
shortly before its name was
changed to the Rex cinema.

Below: Another cinema nearby was
the Palace, almost in the centre of
this 1948 view across Frogmoor,
where a flower bed has replaced
the fountain, scrapped in the
wartime metal drive. The Palace
was built in 1922 to replace a
previous Palace, the town's first
cinema, built on the other side
of Frogmoor in 1909 and burnt
down three years later.

The Dyke was used, unofficially, as a swimming pool in the early 1900s. In 1911, an official swimming bath was opened there, simply a 50-yard section separated from the rest of the water by baulks of timber. This photograph, from a visitor's family album, was taken in the mid-twenties.

The Rye from "The Dyke", High Wycombe

HW.4

The Dyke also offered exercise in rowing boats hired from the council's boathouse at its western end. On one side, the water is open to views of the Rye, while the other side is shaded by the trees of Wendover Way, a strip of land given to the town by the Marquis of Lincolnshire in memory of his son killed in the First World War.

The Rye, in its natural state, is a place of recreation and leisure for all, but this paddling pool, fed with water from the adjacent river Wye, was created in 1930 as a special attraction for children, and an adjacent playground was added a few years later. It was still very popular when this picture was taken in 1948.

If you are interested in purchasing other books published by The History Press, or in case you have difficulty finding any of our books in your local bookshop, you can also place orders directly through our website

www.thehistorypress.co.uk

Printed in Great Britain
by Amazon